European Carpets

European Carpets

Michele Campana

Paul Hamlyn

LONDON · NEW YORK · SYDNEY · TORONTO

Translated by Margaret Crosland from the Italian original

Tappeti d'occidente

©*1966 Fratelli Fabbri Editori, Milan*

This edition © copyright 1969
THE HAMLYN PUBLISHING GROUP LIMITED
LONDON · NEW YORK · SYDNEY · TORONTO
Hamlyn House, Feltham, Middlesex, England

S.B.N. 600012484

Text filmset in Great Britain by
Keyspools Ltd, Golborne

Printed in Italy by
Fratelli Fabbri Editori, Milan

Contents

INTRODUCTION

The extremely ancient woven fabrics known as
carpets originated in the East. Ever since their first
appearance they have been closely linked with the
life of man and, apart from being functional objects,
very quickly became ornamental, often achieving the
stature of works of art. The use of knotting, which
originated in relatively remote times in the East,
distinguishes carpets proper from other kinds of
textiles, making them a distinctive form of textile art.

Eastern carpets gradually became known throughout the world, and their influence was responsible
for the development of Western types, which have
their own separate history. Although descended
from a single stock, the human race split into various
groups; and the Eastern carpet stands in much the
same relationship to the various Western carpets.
Islam and Christian Europe produced two large
families of carpets, clearly distinct and characteristic
of different civilisations, but related in having the
same remote Turkoman origins. The Eastern origin

of European carpets is so indisputable that the first examples made in France in the 17th century were described as '*dits de Turquie*' or '*à la façon de Perse et du Levant*'.

It was the peoples of the East who revealed to the West the physical, aesthetic and intellectual pleasure occasioned by the presence of carpets. Pleasure for the feet as they move silently and softly over a beautiful fabric; pleasure for the eye, which enjoys the effects of the colour and design; and pleasure for the mind, which can follow the thoughts and fantasies suggested by pattern, figure and theme. Westerners drew inspiration from these new and unsuspected sensations for their own productions, which they proved able to enrich with features of their own culture and civilisation.

Arab influence

The presence in Spain of the Arabs and Moors (8th–15th centuries), the Crusades (11th–13th centuries), the travels of Marco Polo (1254–1324), the embassies to Venice (from the 13th century onwards), and the colonial expansion of Portugal beginning in the 14th century, were responsible for the introduction of knotted carpets into Europe. Continued contacts and exchanges with the East produced the desire among Europeans to create as well as possess carpets;

this was how the art of knotting took its place alongside other textile arts, which had already reached a high degree of refinement in the West. The carpets which embellished the houses of the rich and powerful were at first exclusively Eastern in origin, but they were followed by those which were being made in Europe. Skilful European craftsmen, availing themselves of techniques learnt from the East, dedicated themselves to this new art, and succeeded in creating works perfectly in keeping with the taste of their countries.

As they lost their original ingenuous beauty, Eastern carpets declined and as a result changed in accordance with new styles evolved by the culture of Europe. A scrupulous examination of the stylistic canons of all countries and all periods reveals that Western carpets were as important as—sometimes more important than—all other forms of decorative art. This was so above all during the period from the mid-17th to the mid-19th century—that is, the era in which reigning styles were closely related to interior decoration. Western carpets of the time achieved such perfection in taste and harmony of composition that they might be said to have constituted the starting-point for all other art forms.

Mural decoration, furniture, doors, fabrics, the covering of furniture and many other objects intended to adorn or give atmosphere—everything was in harmony with the decorative and figurative composition of carpets. These two centuries were also the most active and flourishing period of carpet production in Europe, when it was transformed into an entirely distinctive artistic expression belonging completely to the European spirit.

From then onwards Western carpets were knotted, and they were made by this method more or less everywhere. But the countries which created examples with a history that can be traced, and worthy of being preserved in museums and collections for the edification and inspiration of posterity, are Spain, Portugal, England and France. Countries like Rumania, Bulgaria, Albania, Tunisia, Morocco—and perhaps Italy too (the products of Valtellina and Sardinia)—were always limited to productions of artisan type, of a regional nature which belongs entirely to folk culture. These lesser products of the West are fairly extensive but without significance for the evolution of taste and styles seen as expressions of the customs and culture of peoples. This book will therefore be concerned with the carpet production of the four countries first mentioned.

SPAIN

The Arabs and Moors began the conquest of the Iberian peninsula in AD 710. Their control over the whole peninsula was short-lived, and for hundreds of

1   Cuenca carpet. Museo Arqueológico Nacional, Madrid.

2, 3 (*Left*) Cuenca carpet. (*Right*) Cuenca carpet (detail).

1   Cuenca carpet. Museo Arqueológico Nacional, Madrid.
In the centre, against a blue background, a rich heraldic crest,
with animals rampant, an eagle, and fortresses surmounted by
a plumed helmet. The composition of the border, which has a
yellow background, and of the four corners which close off
the central field, is definitely derived from Persian carpets.

2   Cuenca carpet. 17th century. Tarica Collection, Paris.
This reproduces the usual motifs of Spanish workshops in
the typical combination of yellow and blue. A stylised land-
scape with houses can be glimpsed in the centre.

3   Cuenca carpet (detail). Museo Nacional de Artes
Decorativas, Madrid. This example has a geometrical decoration and is primitive and naïve in inspiration. It is enhanced
by the yellow and blue which harmonise well with the light
background.

4   Cuenca carpet. 17th century. Tarica Collection, Paris.
The decoration is dense, but harmoniously composed; the
yellow background contrasts effectively with the green and
blue. A coat of arms stands out in the centre and there is a
horseman in each of the corners.

4   Cuenca carpet. 17th century.

years the country was subjected to continuous wars between Moslem and Christian states. Although the advantage fluctuated, on the whole Moslem power declined steadily. At the end of the 15th century the triumph of the united Houses of Aragon and Castile brought the Kingdom of Spain into being, and the Moors were driven from Granada, their last foothold on Spanish soil.

It is a complex and turbulent history, but there were advantages in terms of new artistic and cultural exchanges. The political and social relationships between Christian and Moslem in Spain opened a door between East and West, and in this way Europeans became aware of arts that were extremely ancient but quite new to them. Ceramics and textiles were the European arts that benefited most, being enriched by new techniques and aesthetic concepts.

The knotted carpet

The arrival of the knotted carpet was the greatest revelation, and had a profound effect on European domestic habits and ceremonial. Astonishment, admiration and the desire to possess knotted carpets were the principal incentives which spurred the Spaniards to manufacture their own carpets.

Spain was the first European country to possess

knotted Eastern carpets, the first to learn the technique of making them, the first to distribute them and cause them to be admired throughout the whole of Western Europe. The most ancient surviving examples of Spanish-made carpets are scattered throughout the world; very few remain in Spain. Previously familiar only to a few specialists and collectors, they gradually became better known, notably through a series of exhibitions: the Great International Historical Exhibition in 1892, the Exhibition of Moslem Art held in Munich in 1910, the international exhibitions in Barcelona (1929) and Madrid (1933). One result of the revival of interest in Spanish carpets at the end of the 19th century was the stripping of churches and convents: the most ancient pieces were taken out of the country and are now preserved in museums and private collections. The majority are in the United States and Germany, but after the political upheavals of modern times some of these carpets have acquired new locations and owners and it has become somewhat difficult to trace them.

The technique of knotting used in Spain differed from that used in the East in that the thread which created the pile was a single-warp knot, twisted onto a single even or uneven warp thread (as opposed to the double-warp knot used in Eastern carpets). For this reason, the knots made a zig-zag pile, and a design composed of straight lines could not be given a very clear-cut appearance. Another difference

5   Early carpet from Cuenca. Museo Arqueológico
Nacional, Madrid.

   Cuenca carpet. 19th century. Private collection, Milan.

5   Early carpet from Cuenca. Museo Arqueológico Nacional, Madrid. The heraldic emblem stands out in the centre of the yellow background, and in the field can be seen figures of stylised stars, animals and flowers, all of them clearly Eastern in derivation. Red and blue are the predominant decorative colours.

6   Cuenca carpet. 19th century. Private collection, Milan. A late example, in the centre of which is a bird, an inscription in ancient Castilian and a repeated artichoke motif. These subjects are typical of early Spanish production.

7   Carpet from the Levant. Museo Arqueológico Nacional, Madrid. The yellow and red panels are of Moorish inspiration but have been accommodated to Western taste. They create a perfect framework for the repeated vase motif, and enliven an unusual and exceptionally elegant composition.

8   Carpet from the Levant. Museo Arqueológico Nacional, Madrid. The composition is in Spanish style, with yellow and blue as the basic colours. Little stylised animals are inserted here and there in the pattern.

7   Carpet from the Levant.

lay in the cutting of the thread for the knotting: in the East it was cut after every knot, but in Spain all the threads of the little loops between one knot and the next were cut at once, which meant that the pile of the carpet was levelled at the same time.

This method of working was used to make the best carpets from Cuenca, Letur, Liétor and the most important centre of production of all time, Alcaraz. The Spanish knot was most frequently used, alternating with the Persian or 'Sehna' knot and the Turkish or 'Ghiordes' knot; later the Ghiordes knot entirely replaced first the Spanish knot and then the Sehna knot. Apart from some minor variations, the looms and other tools were the same as those used in the East.

Treatment of the Wool

Wool for the carpets came from sheep and, to a lesser extent, goats—animals found in great numbers in Spain and Portugal. (On rare occasions silk was used, and gold and silver threads were added to complete the elegance of the carpet.) In order to obtain wool as pure and soft as possible, the animals were washed several times in running river-water before shearing; afterwards the sheared wool was washed again in clear, warm water, and then smoothed lightly with oil. These operations were followed by combing and spinning. Apart from white, black and

8   Carpet from the Levant. Museo Arqueológico Nacional, Madrid.

brown, which were used in their natural state without dyeing, colours were obtained from vegetable and insect dyes, great care being taken with the quality of the water and the exposure to the air of the skeins of wool. The basic colours used in Spanish production were red, yellow and blue. By the end of the 19th century, synthetic dyes had replaced the natural colours which had enriched Spanish carpets with a variety of shades and an expressiveness in colour that is unsurpassed. The advent of synthetic dyes affected Eastern carpet-making even more adversely, for there the production of hand-knotted carpets had already been declining for some time.

Spanish carpets are already mentioned in the old Arab chronicles. In his descriptions of Africa and Spain, El Edrisi, the 12th-century geographer, says that at Chinchilla 'they make hangings that cannot be imitated anywhere' and that in this city 'excellent wool carpets are worked by hand'. At this time the region of Murcia was also famous for its carpet-workshops.

In 1255 Eleanor of Castile went to England to marry Edward I and took Eastern and Spanish carpets with her; this was how they became known in Britain. On this occasion the Spanish ambassadors and dignitaries had valuable textiles and carpets hung on the walls of houses and along the streets the wedding procession was to pass through; the church was covered with them. The chronicles of the period speak of them with indescribable enthusiasm. Events of this kind helped to make Europeans aware of this new art form, and the upper classes adapted these products of luxurious and refined 'pagan society' to their own tastes and habits. Carpets everywhere came to be regarded as completely indispensable to an aristocratic way of life.

Spanish production can be divided into four main periods: Arab, Gothic, Renaissance and 18th-century, the last-named foreshadowing the decadence of the 19th century.

The Arab period. The carpets from Alcaraz, Abanilla, Chinchilla and Cuenca belong to the Arab period. The vast majority are no longer to be found anywhere, and the student must be content with descriptions of them by historians and in contemporary inventories of goods. Two carpets are known, with precise details about the period and place of origin: one from the 14th century, with a decidedly Moorish character, once adorned a synagogue and was in recent times taken to the State Museum of Berlin; the other, in the Museum of Granada, was executed with a distinctly Persian technique but is characteristically Hispano-Moresque in its design. Analysis reveals that these Spanish carpets derived directly from Egyptian, Syrian and Arab models: they repeat designs with Coptic motifs, Kufic inscriptions, sphinxes, legendary animals, lions, birds and so on.

9   Carpet from the Levant. Museo Arqueológico Nacional, Madrid.

10 Alcaraz carpet (detail). Early 16th century. Tarica
Collection, Paris.

9   Carpet from the Levant. Museo Arqueológico Nacional, Madrid. The stylised representation of vases and garlands of flowers is effected in blue on a yellow background with the maximum of elegance.

10   Alcaraz carpet (detail). Early 16th century. Tarica Collection, Paris. This knotted carpet, with its blue background, is characterised by motifs inspired by the velvets of the Renaissance. The artichoke theme appears on the panels and stylised chimeras on the border.

11   Alcaraz carpet (detail). Museo Nacional de Artes Decorativas, Madrid. The orange-yellow and blue create a perfectly balanced contrast in colour and tone and the complicated arrangement of the multiple decorative motifs is superbly executed. Also striking is the graphic simplicity of the design on the border.

12   Alcaraz carpet. Museo Nacional de Artes Decorativas, Madrid. The few decorative motifs are of Eastern derivation, and the colours are similar to those of the so-called Damascus carpet, for the light and dark blue tend to be slightly greenish and stand out well in contrast to the red background.

11 Alcaraz carpet (detail).

12 Alcaraz carpet. Museo Nacional de Artes Decorativas,
Madrid.

Green and red predominate, and there is a profusion of gold.

Since Spanish production during the Arab period was insufficient to meet demands from inside and outside the country, many carpets were imported from the East and North Africa. This has given rise to difficulties which are understandable since—technical similarities aside—some Spanish examples rival in quality the finest Eastern carpets. Inventories of the period refer to Turkish, Persian, Berber, Tunisian and other carpets, confusing them with those produced in Spain.

As a rule, the design of these carpets is of the Eastern geometrical type, with borders of vegetable and animal motifs in Western taste. Carpets of this period, more than any other forms of artistic expression, reflect the situation of Spain, divided into small states and held in the grip of two big powers: Islam, with its refinements, its love of the pleasures of life, and its ferocity; and Catholicism, with its rigid and austere puritanism. The relentless wars and splendid court life of Spain both stemmed from the ambitions and interaction of these two forces.

The Gothic period. The oldest group of Spanish carpets proper is called 'El Almirante' because most of them carried the arms of Admiral Enriques and his relatives. The most interesting Spanish examples (those which foreign museums and collectors later fought to possess) came, like many other carpets, from the Convent of Sta Clara of Palencia. The first donation to the convent was made in the will of Doña Juana Mendoza, wife of Don Alfonso Enriquez, Admiral of Castile, and was followed by many bequests from other dignitaries. These carpets are listed in the inventory (1504) of the Catholic King and are called 'old and torn carpets'. Most of them carry arms and blazons—of the Admiral of Castile of the House of Enriquez; of Fadrique Enriquez, Lord of Medina de Rioseco, Admiral of Castile and Count of Melgar and his wife Marina Ayala (the parents of Queen Juana Enriquez, the second wife of Juan II of Aragon); and of Juan de Rojas, Lord of Monzon y Cabia, and his wife Maria Enriquez, younger sister of Fadrique Enriquez. The majority of these extremely interesting 'El Almirante' carpets are now in the Philadelphia Museum of Art and the Museum of Chicago; others are in private collections.

Another group of carpets of the same period, bearing the arms of Maria of Castile, wife of Alfonso V of Aragon (1438–1481), was for a long time kept in the convent of St Isobel in Toledo before their sale to private individuals and consequent dispersal.

A mural in the Palace of the Popes in Avignon is an important contemporary document: there is a carpet in the painting with a design of octagons containing stars and other motifs, typical of Spanish production. This is explained by the fact that Pope

John XXII (1315–1334) took a good number of Spanish carpets with him when he went to Avignon. This is an indication of the popularity they enjoyed among the higher ranks of society. All these examples quoted belong to the so-called 'Gothic' period, which is also that during which Catholicism triumphed over Islam.

The union of Aragon and Castile through the marriage of Ferdinand and Isabella was the effective beginning of the Kingdom of Spain, shortly afterwards followed by the expulsion of the Moors from Granada (1492). Catholic fanaticism—manifested in its most extreme form by the Inquisitors who relentlessly pursued Jews and Moslems—led to the removal of everything characteristically Moorish in the arts. Carpet designs were inspired by the shapes of vegetables; the octagons, which were Moorish in origin, were transformed into laurel wreaths all in one shade of green with red backgrounds. Human and animal figures appear: bears and lions with human heads, people standing at the windows of houses and castles, and so on. Other recurrent motifs include one of five-branched candlesticks and one with Kufic inscriptions, but they were deprived of any religious significance and were regarded only as decorations. One unmistakable characteristic is the repetitive motif (apparently a small-scale honeycomb design) which makes a background pattern to the main design.

A new design of a distinctly Western character was the brocade motif which was later copied everywhere, even in the East. There are carpets with this motif in the Museum of the Escurial; they were described as coming from the Levant (that is, from eastern Spain). Most of them are in shades of green and blue, and were given to the Monastery of the Escurial by Charles V's son Philip II (1556–1598) and his wife Queen Mary of England. The carpets which belonged to the Duke of Lerma—perfect examples of the productions of this period—must also be mentioned.

The most flourishing centres of carpet-manufacture during the Gothic period were the Levant, Cuenca, Alcaraz and Chinchilla. The Arabs, now subjects of Christian Spain, collaborated in the making of these carpets; production was so large that many were exported or made on commission for foreign courts. In the French inventories of the 15th century, Spanish carpets are listed among the possessions of the Bishop of Langres, the Duchess of Berry and Anne of Brittany. Churches were adorned with them and Spanish carpets began to form a part of cathedral treasuries along with other valuable objects.

There is an example with a hunting scene in the Philadelphia Museum of Art; the number of different animals and the richness of the foliage recall the most famous Persian hunting carpets. There is still more evidence of the fame of fine Spanish carpets: in his

13   Alcaraz carpet. Early 16th century. Tarica Collection, Paris.

14   Alcaraz carpet. Museo Nacional de Artes Decorativas,
Madrid.
15   Alcaraz carpet (detail). Museo Nacional de Artes
Decorativas, Madrid.

13   Alcaraz carpet. Early 16th century. Tarica Collection, Paris. The example reproduced follows Arabic designs in the decoration with medallions, and in using red and green.

14   Alcaraz carpet. Museo Nacional de Artes Decorativas, Madrid. The vegetable motifs are typically Spanish, as are the colours (yellow, orange, blue and white), which are juxtaposed with balance and harmony.

15   Alcaraz carpet (detail). Museo Nacional de Artes Decorativas, Madrid. This is a detail of the carpet reproduced in plate 14, which displays the characteristic decoration of the period in all its elegance.

16   Alcaraz carpet (detail). Museo Nacional de Artes Decorativas, Madrid. A carpet that might easily be confused with one from Damascus, since the decoration of the polygons is composed of many small motifs in yellow, red and blue.

16 Alcaraz carpet (detail).

collection of anecdotes, Al Maqqari (16th century) quotes Ben Said and Saqundi as testifying to the beauty of the floral Hispano-Moresque carpets which covered the walls and floors of Spanish houses and were exported to both the East and West.

The Renaissance period. During the Renaissance the taste for Eastern designs and motifs revived. Stylised geometrical motifs and naturalistic, heraldic designs are found separately or in combination. Spanish techniques were abandoned completely and carpets were made with the Turkish Ghiordes knot or (very few) the Persian Sehna knot. Production was intensified, colours became more brilliant—yellow and orange predominating—and carpets became an integral part of the splendour of the Renaissance courts. All the Spanish centres, with Alcaraz at their head, created extremely refined pieces, and the 16th and 17th centuries were the golden age of Spanish carpets. Cuenca became a centre of carpet collections and a market of international importance as well as being a great centre of production.

This is the period of what were known in the West as 'Holbein' carpets, being so called after the great German painter in whose works they featured so often. Apart from some variations in the borders, which are more geometrical in style, they are faithful copies of carpets from Ushak in Anatolia, and are attributed to the Renaissance period because they were so widely distributed then. In fact these carpets appeared somewhat earlier (in the East and in Spain) than Holbein and the many other European painters —especially the Italians—who showed them in their works. An earlier period is clearly indicated by the elegant and beautiful design with arabesques and the happy combination of basic colours in the Spanish carpets (red, yellow and blue); these, needless to say, explain the great favour enjoyed everywhere by Holbein carpets.

The 18th century. The last phase of important Spanish production began early in the century, in Madrid and Cuenca under the protection of the royal family. Contemporary documents refer to carpets made in a tapestry weave rather than by knotting; in the palace inventories of Philip V (1700–1746), the first of the Spanish Bourbons, tapestries (hangings) used on the floors like carpets are mentioned, and these are clearly of the Aubusson type imposed on Spain through the influence of the French Bourbons. But if the Spanish manufacturers imitated French carpets, they reached a high artistic level in this field. These tapestry woven carpets achieved their greatest prestige during the second half of the 18th century when, following the fashion which had been introduced during the reign of Charles III (1759–1788), decoration was in Pompeian taste. (This was the time of the first excavations carried out at Pompeii, of which Charles III was the enthusiastic patron.)

Although production at other places of manufacture began to decline, Cuenca and Madrid remained the most important centres. In Madrid there were many workshops in operation, the most important being the Fábrica Real, which was directed by such craftsmen as Juan Antonio Alencastre, Gabriel José de Estrada and Matias Gonzales. But Cuenca was the most important centre, so much so that the king granted a coat of arms and various privileges to Gaspar Carrion, a master in all the textile arts, for having set up a workshop producing 'carpets in the styles of Turkey, Spain and Messina'. (It should not be forgotten that Sicily had once been subject to the Arabs and was a Spanish possession from the 14th century; there were certainly workshops in Messina in which Saracens and Spaniards worked together.) Carrion founded a school at Cuenca in which the art of knotting was taught to boys while they were still very young. Magnificent carpets were produced by the school; they are now kept in the Town Hall, the Cathedral and the Museum in Cuenca. Each one carries the date, the number of carpets of a given design reproduced, and the seal of the Fábrica Real. But Carrion's activities at Cuenca did not last long, for he did not earn as much as his work deserved. He therefore went to Valencia, where he set up his own private workshop and opened a school of textile arts for boys.

17 Spanish carpet (detail). 17th century. Tarica Collection, Paris.

17   Spanish carpet (detail). 17th century. Tarica Collection, Paris. The texture of this piece is like that of an Aubusson; but it has a poor and hybrid design and colours that do not stand out strongly.

18   Spanish carpet. 16th century. Catan Collection, Paris. Quite an interesting carpet. The beautiful central area illustrates the achievements of Pizarro, conqueror of Peru and founder of the city of Lima. On the border the motif of the Damascan panels is taken up again but is sophisticated with stylised palm leaves. The basic colour is red, from which the green, yellow and blue stand out.

19   Murcia carpet (detail). 15th–16th century. Victoria and Albert Museum, London. Photograph John Webb. The rich design, inspired by decorations on contemporary fabrics, unwinds continuously on the yellow background, creating dense and varied motifs; it is more restrained on the border, where it develops with large stylised motifs.

18   Spanish carpet. 16th century.

PIZARO DEO   HONOR GLORIA

19 Murcia carpet (detail). 15th–16th century. Victoria and Albert Museum, London. Photograph John Webb.

The Archdeacon D. Alfonso Palafox obtained enough money from Charles III to resuscitate carpet production at Cuenca, but this renewed activity lasted not much more than a decade; it continued for a short time afterwards through the work of private individuals such as Benito Canales, Francisco Campos and Manuel Garces.

Production in Madrid continued into the early years of the 19th century mainly through the work of Juan Bautista Stuyck, who petitioned the king and obtained permission to execute cartoons for the carpets produced at Madrid. The object was to give work to a large number of unemployed operatives. The entire output was commissioned to decorate the palace of the Escurial. Very fine carpets, with Berber and Moorish designs, were produced, nearly all of them signed and dated. The work was done under the direction of such master-craftsmen as Juan Antonio Alencastre and Gabriel José de Estrada. The most important examples appear in the inventories of Charles IV (1788–1808) and Ferdinand VII (1814–1833). The majority, however, were lost during a great fire.

Soon after the initiative taken by Stuyck, similar ventures were undertaken by private individuals, and schools for boys became intensely active, though for only a short time. After the first decade of the 19th century, Spanish carpets went into a complete decline. Only Cuenca, directed with tenacity by private individuals, held out for about fifty years.

In about 1900 the Count of Retamoso tried to revive carpet-manufacture, but on the whole he had little success. Wars and political turmoil brought the attempt to an end. The workshops in Cuenca and Madrid were closed and the Spanish carpet existed no longer. Then the Fábrica Nacional de Alfombras continued the work of the Fábrica Real of Madrid and its production was named 'Alpujarra' after a range of mountains in the Sierra Nevada.

This art, once so noble, has now fallen to the level of popular craftsmen's work. Good carpets are still produced, but they do not match the beauty of the old Spanish carpets, whose colours and designs reflected taste and culture from century to century and conjured up the whole tormented history of Spain.

PORTUGAL

Portuguese carpets did not have a long history, and here only a brief but nonetheless indispensable description of them will be attempted. It is impossible to name the places of origin of Portuguese carpets, or even to discuss various specialised kinds of craftsmanship, as can be done when discussing England and France. These carpets were a by-product of the splendid colonial expansion of Portugal, which from the 15th to 17th centuries took men of this great seafaring nation to Africa, America and Asia.

For ethnic and geographical reasons the history of Portugal was closely linked with that of Spain until 1139, the year in which Portugal was transformed from a '*Contea*' into a kingdom. With the conquest of Lisbon in 1147, King Alfonso I (1139–1185) established the basis for a completely autonomous state composed of all the little kingdoms and states which had kept the Iberian peninsula locked in continuous struggles (between themselves or against the Moslem states). It was a long and difficult enterprise, in which the clergy, aristocracy and people willingly collaborated for three centuries, with the common aim of establishing judicial, religious, economic and cultural independence.

National territory extended as far as Algarve and Agarem. Portugal is unique in Europe in that it very quickly acquired boundaries which have remained materially the same right up to the present day. Even the Latin language transformed itself first into 'Romanço', then into Portuguese; and ancient Lusitania became Portugal. Once independence had been secured, the Portuguese spirit required a new form of expression which was to manifest itself in a love of great voyages and the exploration of unknown lands. This impulse was to stir the whole of this strong and noble people.

For a long time Portugal attempted above all to

20   Murcia carpet (detail). 15th–16th century. Victoria and Albert Museum, London. Photograph John Webb.

21 Alcaraz carpet (detail). 17th century. Victoria and Albert Museum, London. Photograph John Webb.

20   Murcia carpet (detail). 15th–16th century. Victoria and Albert Museum, London. Photograph John Webb. This was made with the Spanish knot. On the red background there emerge small panels obviously of Arab-Damascan inspiration with a definite preponderance of green, yellow and blue.

21   Alcaraz carpet (detail). 17th century. Victoria and Albert Museum, London. Photograph John Webb. The central field, composed of dense, frequently repeated motifs, is reminiscent of the Persian Feragan type of carpet. The border, more spaciously designed and elegant than the background, is certainly Spanish in inspiration.

22   Goa carpet. 18th century. Angelo Frova Collection, Milan. A beautiful carpet with a red background which brings out the white and yellow decoration. It contains animal designs, notably six superb lions with human faces.

23   Portuguese carpet, dated 1680. Mayorcas Collection, London. This was made with a needle and has a floral design and the typical mustard-coloured background in which a strong blue predominates.

22   Goa carpet. 18th century.

defend herself against immediate dangers, allying variously with Spain, France and England against the Moslem peril. As a result, a great and powerful fleet began to be formed. Lisbon, a strategically placed port of call between the Mediterranean and the North Sea, was also well-situated for searching for new lands which promised adventure and lucrative commercial opportunities.

In the early 15th century John of Aviz made peace with Castile, ending a long and costly conflict; and at the same time the Portuguese captured Ceuta in Morocco (1415), thus checking Arab expansion towards Gibraltar. With security at home, the successful period of Portuguese colonial expansion and discoveries began: in 1418 Porto Santo, in 1419 Madeira, in 1424 Grand Canary, in 1427 the Azores. In 1433 Gil Eanes went round Cape Bojador; and in 1444 Cape Verde was reached. These were steps towards a new world, to which Portugal's intelligent and far-sighted colonial policy brought the benefits of Western civilisation. In 1471, after their conquest of Tangiers, the Portuguese developed an ambition to possess the North African coast, and the great plan to reach India by crossing Africa took shape. At the same time the Portuguese were reaching across the Atlantic. In 1460 they reached Santiago, Fogo and Mayo, and in 1500 Cabral discovered Brazil, which became the most flourishing of the Portuguese colonies and remained in her possession until 1822.

23 Portuguese carpet, dated 1680. Mayorcas Collection, London.

In 1486 Bartolomeo Dias rounded the Cape of Good Hope seeking the sea route to India; this was a project never abandoned by the Portuguese, or by the Venetians and the Genoese, whom the Turks barred from contact with India overland. In 1498 Vasco da Gama discovered the sea route to India, and in 1499 Goa became the centre of all Portuguese colonising activity, the territory becoming known as 'the Eastern Empire'.

In the countries they conquered, the Portuguese did not slaughter or abuse their power, but brought European techniques and refinements with them, introducing agrarian reforms and building roads, houses and schools. The diffusion of European culture and Christianity was to a great extent the work of missionaries, and the most important part was played by the Society of Jesus. As a result, Portuguese is still the official language of Portugal's ex-colonial possessions.

Portuguese colonists rarely penetrated into the interior. This great seafaring people tended to occupy the coasts, along which they established scattered fortresses and posts; the *feitorias* were like a long chain of sea-shore defences which prevented enemies from disembarking, guaranteed access to the sea and maintained the commercial hegemony of the various ports of call. The Portuguese were almost always assisted by the natives, who viewed them as beneficent, superior beings rather than intruders.

In 1510 Alfonso de Albuquerque took Malacca for
Portugal, making the first European contact with
China. The development of Portuguese commerce
was enormous, and every European nation both
feared and envied Portuguese power. But although
her fleet was the most powerful in the world, the
country—small in size and population—found the
burden of her vast Eastern Empire more and more
difficult to bear. The Portuguese always found
themselves faced by English and Dutch ships anxious
to snatch the territories and seas they had conquered;
and Spain, which had become powerful after the expulsion of the Arabs and the union of the states of
Leon, Navarre, Castile and Aragon, applied constant
pressure in the Iberian peninsula itself.

Philip II of Spain (1556–1598) annexed Portugal
in 1580. The decline of the Eastern Empire dates
from this period. England's victory over the 'Invin-
cible Armada' of Spanish and Portuguese ships
(1588) was a heavy blow. The re-establishment of
Portugal's independence and accession of a Portuguese king, John IV of Braganza (1640–1656), did
little to improve the country's international situation. Her Asiatic and African possessions diminished
inexorably, and only Brazil seemed secure. In spite
of the achievements of the missionaries the sun was
soon due to set on the once glorious empire of this
maritime power.

In order to sustain her commerce, Portugal tried

24 Portuguese carpet. 17th century. Tarica Collection, Paris.

25 Portuguese carpet. 18th century. Patani Collection, Milan.

24   Portuguese carpet. 17th century. Tarica Collection, Paris. In beige, blue and mustard, this carpet has a large arabesque with floral motifs.

25   Portuguese carpet. 18th century. Patani Collection, Milan. Made with a needle and big stitches; the colours are a typical combination of mustard, light blue and white. The simplicity of the design, employing a minimum of decorative elements, makes it extremely attractive.

26   Portuguese carpet. 17th century. Tarica Collection, Paris. In floral style but richly ornamented with animals, peacocks, birds, dragons, etc. As usual there is a strong preponderance of yellow and blue.

27   Portuguese carpet. 18th century. Mayorcas Collection, London. This example, made on a loom, has dense decoration on the background as well as on the border, and is sometimes Oriental and sometimes Western in taste; there is a preponderance of yellow and blue. It was commissioned in 1747 by the Convento da Regeneracáo Religiosas in Braga.

27 Portuguese carpet. 18th century. Mayorcas Collection, London.

throughout the 18th century to continue her work of colonisation, and attempted to create a large Brazilian and African empire of small autonomous states under Portuguese hegemony. But the French Revolution and Napoleonic wars ushered in a period of internal upheavals and foreign interventions during which Brazil broke away from Portugal. Once the terrible political and financial crisis of 1890 was over there was an attempt to reform the country's political life, but continual disorders and party struggles led to the downfall of the House of Braganza and the setting up of a republican constitution in 1910. Some kind of stability was achieved only in the 1920s. Even so, a considerable number of possessions in Africa remained (São Thomé, Principe, Cape Verde, Guinea, Angola and Mozambique); and in Asia, Portugal held Goa, Diu, Damão, Macao and part of Timor.

The 'Portuguese' Carpet

Such a historical outline may at first seem superfluous in a book of this sort. It is, however, essential to the understanding of the 'Portuguese' Carpet, for this was never in fact manufactured in Portugal. It was a product of the countries occupied by the Portuguese, for the conquerors took over local production and also had carpets made on commission. (Local production is not dealt with here, since it belongs to types already described in a preceding volume.) Commissioned carpets, whether made in Portugal by Moslem workers or by natives in the East, were enriched with—sometimes spoiled by—details imposed by the person who commissioned the carpet. Some details are fairly close to Spanish and Arab–Moorish taste, with designs that are smaller and denser. The best known examples are from Goa, not because there was a particular type of production there to cater for the Portuguese, but because Goa was always the most important and active of Portuguese colonies. It was the place where all the commercial and artistic interests of the vast Eastern Empire came together.

During the second half of the 15th century, the painters Nuno Gonçalves and Alvaro Pires were active as designers of tapestries and carpets. Portuguese tapestries were not made in Portugal either, but were commissioned from Flanders. The carpets were produced in Africa and Asia—but for a few made in Portugal—by Moslems.

At the beginning of the 16th century, during the golden age of Portugal, there were other active and quite well-known painters, for example Cristovao de Figueiredo, Sanches Coehlo and Jorge Alfonso, who was nominated as the king's General Superintendent of the Fine Arts. Carpets kept their place of honour among them, since relations with exotic lands had led

to their becoming objects of use as well as *objets d'art*.
In the many ships of the Portuguese fleet carpets came
first on the list of equipment. They were important
as articles of exchange and also as gifts.

After the first half of the 16th century Portuguese
carpets display a new feature, resulting from contact
with Japan: the decorative motifs of the Far East
were added to those of the Arabs and Spaniards.
Fernão Mendes Pinto, a Jesuit, went to Japan on
several occasions and brought back objects indicative of the existence of a very different civilisation.
In 1541 Pero de Faria was appointed Governor of
Malacca, and thereafter Asiatic influence was felt
even more strongly in the design of carpets. The
Portuguese had them made wherever they traded
and colonised, which is why it is not easy to recognise
a carpet as specifically Portuguese.

After the 16th century the star of Portugal began
to fade. The Portuguese carpet too began to decline.
Goa was the colony which continued to flourish for
the longest time and to send carpets executed on
commission to the West. During the 17th century
representations of seascapes showing sailing-ships
and people occurred frequently, and figurative
representation was carried out with great precision
of detail. It seemed as though the Portuguese,
conscious of their declining greatness, wanted to
perpetuate the seafaring epoch of their history on
their carpets, leaving a record more lively and telling

than written accounts. Nowhere are the great Portuguese adventures better evoked than in their carpets, since only in these are immediacy and contemporaneity combined with the exoticism native to the empire won as a result of these adventures.

The type of carpet produced in Portugal during its annexation by Spain (1580–1640) was similar to those made in Spain. There are, however, examples of 17th-century work of Asiatic or African origin which are quite pleasing and elegant. These employ Moorish and Chinese motifs, but also reproduce figurative designs that are typically Portuguese; their decorative composition exemplifies the great cultural and artistic past of Portugal. Such carpets are, regrettably, rare, and only a connoisseur is capable of identifying them.

By the 19th century the Portuguese carpet had to all intents and purposes ceased to be produced. Very few examples still exist, since the famous earthquake which devastated Portugal in 1755 destroyed a great part of her artistic heritage.

ENGLAND

The word 'carpet', meaning a woven fabric which covers and decorates the floor and protects against the cold, was almost unknown in England until little less than seven centuries ago. The functions of protection

28 Axminster carpet (detail). 18th century. Victoria and
Albert Museum, London. Photograph John Webb.

28   Axminster carpet (detail). 18th century. Victoria and
Albert Museum, London. Photograph John Webb. Carpet
made with the Ghiordes knot in a typical French style and
with geometrical details on the border.

29   Exeter carpet (detail), dated 1757. Victoria and Albert
Museum, London. Photograph John Webb. Another carpet
made with the Turkish Ghiordes knot and inspired by the
French. The shell motif with a human face is typical; note the
superb basket of flowers on the red table cloth.

30   English carpet, dated 1760. Mayorcas Collection,
London. This was made with a needle with typical designs
of the type described as George III. The colours are very soft.

31   Axminster carpet (detail). 19th century. Victoria and
Albert Museum, London. Photograph John Webb. Made
with a needle, with a dark background on which the light
colours stand out. The flower motifs are dense and rich.

29   Exeter carpet (detail), dated 1757.

EXON·IDI

30 English carpet, dated 1760. Mayorcas Collection,
London.

31 Axminster carpet (detail). 19th century. Victoria and
Albert Museum, London. Photograph John Webb.

and decoration were performed only by vegetable matter scattered on the ground: hay, leaves and scented grasses, soft rushes, sheaves of Indian corn and, on special occasions, flower petals. These were the carpets traditionally used in Britain, which, as soon as they had withered, were thrown out of the windows in the most casual way. Before carpets proper were used in the houses of the nobility, the skins of animals were placed on the floor. Later, softer and more flexible rushes were woven together. In this way the first mats were introduced; and although rough and primitive, they anticipated the carpet in that they too were functional man-made objects.

The Crusaders brought the first Eastern carpets to England. Then, in 1255, the marriage of Eleanor of Castile and Edward I of England led to the use of Spanish carpets. The Queen's possessions included many rare carpets of matchless beauty, and the ambassadors and dignitaries who accompanied her to England brought carpets of a type and quality never before seen in England as gifts to the court. These were the models which inspired the English and led to the making of English carpets; for three centuries —the 16th to the 19th—these carpets were admired and sought after all over the world. They were the final achievements of a type of English art that was very old and already known everywhere: the art of embroidery.

Opus Anglicanum

'Opus Anglicanum' was the name by which English embroidery was known; its origin is to be found far back in the past, and it was known and appreciated all over Europe in the Middle Ages. It was carried out on embroidery frames and reached a high level of artistry, surpassing painting in artistic and documentary value. The detailed figurative designs constitute an important source for the political and religious history of the nation, and are filled with strong patriotic feeling. The fineness of the execution and the materials employed (wool, linen, silk, gold and silver), and the beauty of the colours and purity of the designs contributed to the creation of these masterpieces. Some idea of the importance of the subject may be gained from reading these words of the French archaeologist Laborde: 'I know of no greater service that can be rendered to the arts than that of writing the history of embroidery. This would not be a complementary study but an introduction to the history of painting.'

Opus Anglicanum represents the most refined and complete expression of Medieval English art. It includes the most varied types of objects, intended both for use and decoration, which provide valuable illustrations of customs and events of national and world importance. The most interesting period of Opus Anglicanum is that of the High Middle Ages;

32　English carpet, dated 1805. Mayorcas Collection, London.

33　English carpet. 19th century. The Vigo Art Galleries, London.

32   English carpet, dated 1805. Mayorcas Collection, London. This carpet belongs to the George III period and was made with a needle. The rose motif is very accurately and successfully reproduced on an ochre background.

33   English carpet. 19th century. The Vigo Art Galleries, London. This carpet is knotted; the floral decoration, predominantly yellow and red, stands on a light background and is arranged to form of a kind of asymmetrical centre.

34   English carpet. 19th century. The Vigo Art Galleries, London. Knotted, with a yellow background and rich floral decoration in very light colours.

35   English carpet. 19th century. The Vigo Art Galleries, London. This was made with the Turkish knot, in light tones on a pink background and with French decoration and large rosettes in the centre.

34   English carpet. 19th century.

its style is permeated with the spirit of its Norman origins, completely untouched by influences from other styles and other civilisations.

The extreme fineness of the needlework enhanced the figurative composition even further, and each object became outstanding of its kind. Banners, vestments, hangings, bedspreads and other items sold rapidly all over Europe and were among the most treasured gifts anyone could give. During the 12th century Popes Adrian IV, Urban IV, Innocent IV and Boniface VIII received from ambassadors and sovereigns gifts of embroidery originally from England which were truly works of art. Fabrics or fragments of fabrics are to be found in Italy at Anagni, Ascoli, Pienza, Bologna and Rome; in France at St Bertrand de Comminges and Rennes; in Belgium at Tournai, and in Spain at Toledo.

Opus Anglicanum had a lasting influence not only on English embroidery, but also on English carpets, in spite of influences from France, Flanders and Asia.

The 16th Century

Although, as already pointed out, it was the Crusaders and Eleanor of Castile who introduced Oriental carpets into England, their first widespread use in

35 English carpet. 19th century. The Vigo Art Galleries, London.

English houses began during the reign of Henry VIII (1509–1547). Indeed, Henry VIII seems to have been an enthusiastic collector, and a Holbein portrait shows him standing on a Turkish Ushak rug. Less extravagant owners used their carpets as covers for tables, cupboards and chests rather than for floor coverings, as can be seen in paintings of the period.

The formation of the great English trading companies meant that journeys to the Near and Far East became even more frequent. The formation of the Muscovy Company (1555) to trade along the shores of the White Sea meant that English merchants reached Moscow; from there, across the Volga and the Caspian, they travelled to Persia, where they bought carpets, and English weavers were enabled to learn the ancient art of knotting. The Turks, on the other hand, were aware of the danger to what had always been an Eastern monopoly, and refused any contact with the English. In order to further commerce with the East, Queen Elizabeth (1558–1603) chartered the East India Company in 1601.

Extensive economic and cultural interests were created in this way, and the art of the carpet, and appreciation of carpets, developed rapidly.

It was the arrival of Eastern carpets in great numbers that stimulated the English to make their own. English carpets were of two main types, and were made either on looms or on embroidery frames. Loom-woven carpets were usually made with the

Turkish knot in wool on a linen ground, and depended
largely on the motifs of Eastern carpets. Sometimes,
however, coats of arms and dates were also incor-
porated. Embroidered carpets were made on a frame
with a needle on a canvas ground, and the influence
of Opus Anglicanum can still be seen in the floral and
abstract designs.

Carpet making was work that could be carried out
by people of any class, and was at first entirely a matter
of initiative taken by private individuals. There were
merchants who had carpets made by craftsmen at
their own expense, but the workshops concerned
were always on a modest scale. Large workshops
came into being later when the art was on the point
of decline.

Among the carpets for tables and floors which
survived from this period are some in the Anatolian
taste (easily mistaken for genuine Middle Eastern
products) made at the same time as characteristically
English pieces.

People of all classes and occupations applied themselves to carpet making. Ordinary working people
owned looms on which fabrics and carpets could be
woven. And no aristocratic home was without a tutor
—sometimes more than one—who would teach the
young girls the art of embroidery and needlework,
an essential in the education of any high born lady.

Queen Elizabeth spent many hours at her embroidery frame, setting an example which the ladies

of her court imitated, competing to create the most varied objects.

The works made by Mary Queen of Scots (1524–1587) during her long imprisonment are unmistakably English. Objects of the most varied type (among them some carpets) carry her emblems and mottoes, and bear witness to the hours and hours of solitude endured by this unfortunate woman. They also show the esteem in which work on the loom was held in England. Shakespeare himself extols the products of the loom as objects worthy of the highest consideration.

When Queen Elizabeth died in 1603 the decorative arts in England were under very strong Chinese influence, and this was also reflected in carpets. These were either knotted or worked with a needle. It was the period of petit point, which had been learnt from the French and was worked in wool on canvas. The dark background appears again and mythological subjects now attracted people of all classes, enabling the executants to demonstrate their familiarity with classical antiquity.

Alongside work of this type can be seen designs with flowers and animals, extremely rich in variety and detail. This was caused mainly by the spread of the early published herbals, which are still of great scientific interest. Among the most important are the *Grete Herball* which is thought to date from 1516 and prompted the herbal of Richard Banckes (1525),

36 Axminster carpet (detail). 19th century. C. John Collection, London.

36   Axminster carpet (detail). 19th century. C. John Collection, London. A knotted carpet, with an intense yellow background and decoration in white, blue and a few touches of red. The composition is floral but with reminiscences of Eastern design mingled with motifs in Western taste.

37   Axminster carpet (detail). 19th century. C. John Collection, London. Another knotted carpet, the decoration including a mixture of French and Eastern motifs. Blue is used a great deal on the yellow background in the centre. There is a dark background on the borders, from which the repeated geometrical pattern with rich floral motifs stands out.

38   Axminster carpet (detail). 19th century. The Vigo Art Galleries, London. A knotted carpet with splendid recherché decoration, similar to that of the Savonnerie carpets and brought into relief by the brick-coloured background.

39   Axminster carpet (detail). 19th century. The Vigo Art Galleries, London. Made with the Turkish knot, with a brick-coloured background and white and yellow decorations. It was definitely inspired by French models and could easily be confused with a Savonnerie carpet.

37   Axminster carpet (detail). 19th century.

38 Axminster carpet (detail). 19th century. The Vigo Art Galleries, London.

39 Axminster carpet (detail). 19th century. The Vigo Art
Galleries, London.

the *Catalogus Plantarum* (1542) of Konrad von Gesner, the *Historia Animalium* which was published in Switzerland in 1558, the *New Herbal* of William Turner which appeared between 1551 and 1562, and Gerard's herbal of 1597. Exotic and rare flowers and strange animals were reproduced in embroidery and on carpets, which were produced in larger quantities than ever and were immensely popular at home and abroad.

The influence of French refugees

After the Massacre of St Bartholomew (1572) many refugees fled from France to England, and they helped to spread a taste for the woven portrait, which was then fashionable on the Continent. The woven portrait does not belong to the genre of carpets proper, but to the broad class of objects made with a needle. It is referred to here because the execution and design is exactly the same as on carpets worked on an embroidery frame. In these the taste displayed is decidedly Western. The human and animal figures, and the floral decoration which enriches both heraldic devices and the hunting scenes filled with legendary animals, contain elements strongly reminiscent of Italian Renaissance motifs; at the same time the frequent appearance of English armorial bearings

and mottoes, and the use of certain shades of colour
—sometimes delicate and sometimes intense—
demonstrate that these carpets are products of English
craftsmanship.

The 18th century

In the 18th century there was a return to the Gothic
style, but the elegant composition and fine colours of
Aubusson and Savonnerie carpets very soon won the
day for the new French styles. The revocation by
Louis XIV (1643–1715) of the Edict of Nantes, which
had granted toleration to the Huguenots (French
Protestants), caused a large-scale emigration to
England. The refugees acted as carriers of French
taste, and for a time it reigned supreme, especially
in carpets. At the same time copies of Eastern models
continued to be worked; there are some examples
from the second half of the 17th century in Pembroke
College, Cambridge, and in the library of Wadham
College, Oxford.

This was also the period in which Chinese designs
—first seen during the reign of Elizabeth—became
widely known and imitated. During the early 18th
century the 'Chinese' style was so highly developed
in all forms of decoration that English *chinoiserie*
comprised in effect a separate style complete with

40 English carpet. 19th century. Mayorcas Collection, London.

41 ̇English carpet (detail). 19th century. Mayorcas Collection, London.

40   English carpet. 19th century. Mayorcas Collection, London. This is typically Victorian, made with a needle. The squares contain floral motifs, have backgrounds of yellow or brown, and are separated by lions rampant.

41   English carpet (detail). 19th century. Mayorcas Collection, London. This was made with a needle and is rich with naturalistic floral motifs in many colours, both dark and light.

42   Carpet with geographical map. Early 19th century. Conte Enrico Zeri Collection, Paris. This was made in Turkey but is included because it was made to fulfil an English order in accordance with English models. Apart from the writing, it is reminiscent of examples fashionable in England during the 17th century.

43   French carpet, dated MDC (1600). Catan Collection, Paris. An interesting carpet which repeats on the borders the fortress, initials and knotted bow motif in the centre. The rich, minute and meticulous design is remarkable.

44   Savonnerie carpet, from Gobelins. 17th century. Catan Collection, Paris. The rich floral decoration fills the background and borders with various colours, green predominating. Louis XIII period.

42 Carpet with geographical map. Early 19th century.

43

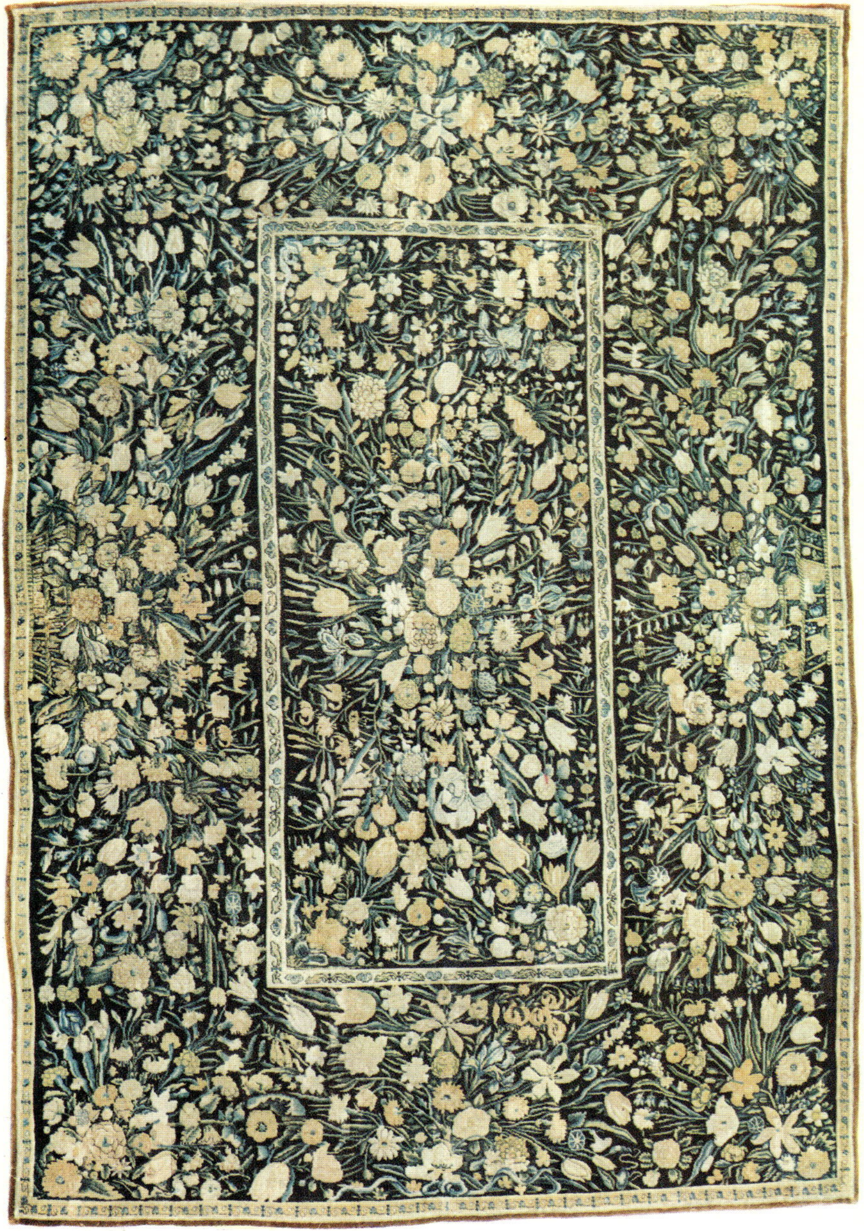

44 Savonnerie carpet from Gobelins. 17th century. Catan Collection, Paris.

43 French carpet, dated MDC (1600). Catan Collection, Paris.

rules and canons. Furniture, ceramics and carpets
were all executed in this new style.

Queen Anne (1702–1714), like previous queens,
enjoyed embroidery and, following her example,
ladies took a pride in sitting at the embroidery frame
in public, working at embroidery and carpet-making
during receptions and the hours of conversation.
Carpets were made in wool, silk, cotton and linen,
their borders carrying inscriptions and showing a
return to naturalism in their designs. A fashion for
carpets which reproduced maps and geographical
charts was launched; it lasted until the second half
of the 18th century and was imitated for a time even
in the Middle East. Workshops in England date only
from the second half of the 18th century. Until that
time commissioned work was usually carried out by
Eastern workers paid by English merchants who
had organised a few centres in the East for production
and collection. The best known English workshops
were those of Paddington, Fulham, Moorfields,
Exeter and Axminster. In 1756 the Royal Society of
Arts instituted prizes for the best carpets produced.
Carpets of Turkish type were made in vivid, brilliant
colours, often on a green background and with
decoration of Eastern inspiration. The majority of
18th-century English carpets were made with the
Ghiordes knot, bear English heraldic devices and
are usually dated, and are therefore not difficult to
recognise.

In the late 18th–early 19th century Chinese, Moorish and Hindu motifs were revived, but this did not last long: French modes became fashionable again and imposed the Aubusson and Savonnerie models. These were followed by the new Directoire and Empire styles (overlapping with decorations in the Pompeian style) which were taken up by British carpet-makers. The apotheosis of the English carpet occurred at this period—which was also the prelude to decline: the first sewing-machines and mechanical looms were at hand.

The first sewing-machine was French and was manufactured in 1834 at Mulhouse in Alsace. The first English machine was patented in 1849.

In 1872 the Royal School of Needlework was founded to combat the threatened decline of the art of embroidery and hand-loom weaving. Thanks to the teaching at the School, carpets and embroidery of a high artistic level continued to be produced. But for a short time only; mechanisation received a fresh impetus with the development of synthetic dyes. In 1856 Perkins discovered how to use aniline purple; in 1869 colours with a chemical base were used for the first time; and in 1879 synthetic indigo was manufactured.

This meant the end of the hand-woven carpet in England and the birth of the machine-made carpet—

which, however, remained characteristically English. Beautiful and elegant moquettes with continuous designs appeared, which in the late 19th and early 20th century matched furniture and prints so well; discreet and delicate in colouring and design, they preserve the English qualities of aristocratic tone, understatement and attachment to tradition. These moquettes are unmistakably English and bear traces of the traditions of Opus Anglicanum, and petit point.

FRANCE

From the reign of Louis XIV, the Sun King, until the Belle Epoque which brought the 19th century to a glorious close, France was synonymous with elegance, refinement and culture. In Europe everything French was fashionable. All the forms of French art were controlled by precisely formulated aesthetic laws and canons, and had evolved along similar lines—literature, music, painting and the decorative arts eventually reaching a point at which they were in effect facets of a single coherent style. The carpet was, in a sense, the meeting-point—the synthesis—of all the arts.

Despite its derivation from Eastern, Spanish and English sources, the French carpet became the expression of a completely national culture. It

45 St-Cyr carpet. 17th century. Catan Collection, Paris.

45   St-Cyr carpet. 17th century. Catan Collection, Paris. Made with a needle, and composed of medallions with mythological, animal and floral scenes. The background is red and the colours of the decorations fairly varied. Régence period.

46   Savonnerie carpet. 17th century. Musée National, Versailles. This was made for the 'Great Pulpit' in the Chapel at Versailles. The French emblems, the three lilies in a gilt bronze colour on the blue background, the royal crown between the two wings of an eagle, and the King's initials, are prominent. The decoration of the background is magnificent.

46   Savonnerie carpet. 17th century.

47   Savonnerie carpet. 17th century. Catan Collection, Paris.
This example comes from Gobelins; the war-like subject, with
arms and helmet, stands out on the floral background. The
basic colour is dark, against which yellow, blue and green
predominate. Louis XIV period.

48   Savonnerie carpet (detail). 18th century. By kind permission of the Royal Collection, Stockholm. This was made
for Louis XV's Banqueting Hall at Versailles and given to
Gustavus III of Sweden by Louis XVI in 1784. It is typical of
the decorative taste of the period.

47 Savonnerie carpet. 17th century. Catan Collection, Paris.

48   Savonnerie carpet (detail). 18th century. By kind
permission of the Royal Collection, Stockholm.

complemented and brought into harmony paintings, furniture, *objets d'art,* ceilings, walls, the very men and women who moved through this ambience. Such men and women were dominated by the cult of elegance, and followed a mode of life which made any other surroundings unthinkable. Even at this point in time it is impossible to visualise their cultural life, even their dress, removed from the setting—the decor—of polite society.

In France, as in other European states, Eastern carpets became known and used as a result of the Crusades, wars, dynastic alliances and diplomatic intrigues which had brought East and West into contact over the centuries. But until relatively late, carpets were always imported—from the East or (later) from Spain and England. In the 15th century there were groups of workers skilled in the process of knotting called *'Tapisseriers Sarrazinois'* who made *'Tapis dits de Turquie',* copying the carpets of the Middle East in their design and method of work. Production was, however, on a small scale and did not last long.

The 17th-century beginnings

The most important French workshops came into being during the reign of Henri IV of Navarre (1589–1610), founder of the Bourbon dynasty. On his succession the country was exhausted by the war against Spain and the wars of religion between Catholics and Protestants, prolonged and complicated by the rivalries between the Valois, Guise and Bourbon families. In order to revive commerce and industry Jean Fortier of Melun had proposed the setting-up of workshops for the manufacture of knotted carpets. It was, however, Pierre Dupont who obtained the King's support and in 1608 opened a workshop beneath the Galerie du Louvre, where various craftsmen and artists were already working for the court.

The first production belonged to the genre described as '*Tapis à la façon du Levant et façon de Turquie*', which Pierre Dupont later made famous in a treatise, *De la Stramatourgie,* which appeared in 1632; in it he stated that he had found a method of imitating the Eastern techniques.

In 1627 Simon Lourdet, Dupont's ex-pupil and partner, set up a new carpet workshop on the outskirts of Paris, in the Hospice de la Savonnerie at Chaillot.

These were the beginnings of the French carpet industry, and owed their existence to the interest shown by Henri IV, and by Louis XIII (1610–1643) and Louis XIV (1643–1715), who were always anxious to provide incentives for industry and commerce. This was the period in which the great tapestry workshops—which played such an im-

portant part in the birth of the French carpet industry
—were set up. Nothing was left to private initiative,
since textile manufacture was a state monopoly. That
is why the products were all of the highest artistic
merit, extremely refined in taste, and very large.

In 1627 Savonnerie came into being, in 1662 the
Manufacture Royale des Gobelins, in 1664 the
Manufacture de Beauvais and in 1665 the Manufacture Royale d'Aubusson. Tapestries were produced which were the source of the two great families
of French carpets, Savonnerie and Aubusson. This
production no longer owed anything to Eastern
carpets, which the French had already more or less
abandoned. With the intention of creating a native
industry, a decree of 17 April 1627 provided the
first French factory with a constitution of eleven
articles, one of which prohibited the importation of
Eastern carpets into France. Carpets took over the
documentary function of tapestry, which recorded
events with vivacity and great detail. The softness of
the material made this possible.

A treatise of the period illustrates with copious
details two splendid series of tapestries, *The Four
Seasons* and *The Four Elements,* made at Gobelins for
the Sun King from cartoons by the painter Lebrun.
In the treatise Pieter van den Berge wrote: 'When
men discovered the art of making verses, they·used
this noble means of expression only to speak of God,
and believed that Poetry, being a divine language,

should serve only to sing His praises. Following this example, we seek other expressions today in order to speak of the August Person of His Majesty—expressions different from those used until now—and new forms in which to describe the great deeds of the greatest of kings.'

The new expressions and forms were tapestries in which allegory and symbolism were employed to convey the munificence of Louis XIV, the patron and protector of the arts. 'Summer', within an oval frame supported by Apollo and Minerva, shows the building of the Palace of the Louvre; the workmen engaged on it are presided over by Apollo, while Minerva presides over those executing tapestries and carpets for the palace. It is an interesting document in the history of the French carpet, and is additional proof of the high esteem in which it was held.

Savonnerie and Aubusson carpets contain the same elements as those used in tapestry to glorify the king. The eagle, the falcon and the lion, synonymous with courage and strength; the shepherd's crook with which the pastor conducts his flock; the horn, with which fame is broadcast; the pomegranate, which holds treasures of wisdom and kindness; and, most important of all, the lily, the symbol of the Royal House of France.

In 'Winter' (*The Four Seasons*), incidentally, Saturn upholds a frame in which the great palaces built by the Sun King are depicted—and they are, of course,

49   St-Cyr carpet. 17th century. Catan Collection, Paris.

50   Savonnerie carpet from Gobelins (detail). 17th century.
Catan Collection, Paris.

49   St-Cyr carpet. 17th century. Catan Collection, Paris. This carpet is rich in decorative elements; in the centre are the royal initials surmounted by the crown, in fairly light colours with a predominance of orange and pink. Régence period.

50   Savonnerie carpet from Gobelins (detail). 17th century. Catan Collection, Paris. The field is almost entirely taken up by the centre, which has a green background. The decoration is interwoven with elegant, contrasting designs in red and beige. Régence period.

51   Savonnerie carpet. 18th century. Catan Collection, Paris. The typical key pattern on the border is of Eastern inspiration; the lyres in the four corners on a blue background are very expressively rendered. Louis XVI period.

52   Savonnerie carpet. 17th century. Catan Collection, Paris. An ornate piece with a dark background. In the centre is a pearl surrounded by lavish decoration; and at the ends are tables covered by cloths and carrying baskets of fruit. Régence period.

51　Savonnerie carpet. 18th century. Catan Collection, Paris.

52 Savonnerie carpet. 17th century. Catan Collection, Paris.

the very palaces which provided such splendid settings for carpets of the period.

For about three centuries, carpets entirely and characteristically French were produced, and for a time they also provided a model for English and Eastern carpets. In the late 18th and early 19th centuries many English carpets similar to the French are to be found; and many Caucasian (Karabak), Turkish (Ghiordes and Melas) and sometimes even Persian (Bidjar) examples have very French motifs integrated in extremely elegant fashion with those of the East. The cause was not so much the export of French carpets to the East as the arrival in France of Eastern craftsmen skilled in knotting. When such craftsmen went back to their own countries they took with them models of French designs which they blended with their own, achieving unusual and pleasing effects.

Even in modern times we find faithful Asian copies of French carpets, called for example 'Indian Aubussons' or 'Chinese Savonneries'. Although these are hybrids and display the bad taste characteristic of servile copies of the past, they bear witness to the supremacy of French styles as models of absolute elegance. Even today, when there is intense competition from new or revived fashions, French taste— though no longer supreme—still provides the criteria by which other carpets are judged.

To appreciate French carpets to the full, it is necessary to imagine them in the splendour of the palaces for which they were made, blending in perfect harmony with their surroundings—part of a total visual experience beginning with the architecture of the exterior and culminating in the lavish detail of the interior. The Tuileries, St Cloud, the Louvre, Versailles, Compiègne, Fontainebleau, might have been created on purpose to receive these superb carpets with all honour.

The contribution to decor

Although some French carpet designers were inspired by these superb palaces, other artists started out to create a decor in accordance with the aesthetic precepts which the designers of the Savonnerie and Aubusson carpets were developing at the same time. These latter designers were naturally following the development of historic national events, and in this way three centuries of French history are closely and consistently reflected in three centuries of the history of art. The 'fame' surrounding the ornamentation in French carpets resembles the decoration in the palaces for which they were destined; the designs and stucco work on ceilings, the decoration of wall panels and the shape and ornamentation of doors take their motifs from the design of the carpets. It was furniture, however, that matched carpets better than anything else. Furniture was made to be placed in immediate

53 Savonnerie carpet. First half of the 17th century. Tarica Collection, Paris.

53   Savonnerie carpet. First half of the 17th century. Tarica Collection, Paris. This is a knotted carpet, with rich floral designs in the centre, bands of geometrical motifs at the ends and a decorative network effect typical of the Régence period.

54   Savonnerie carpet. 18th century. Catan Collection, Paris. A sumptuous carpet indicative of the luxury of the period. Fairly light colours alternate with dark ones. Louis XV period.

55   Savonnerie carpet. 18th century. Musée National, Versailles. This was made for the alcove in the bedroom of Maria Leszcynska, Louis XV's queen. It is enhanced with rich decorative motifs which are developed on a dark background, and has interlaced initials in the corners.

56   Savonnerie carpet (detail). Early 19th century. Catan Collection, Paris. The light-coloured centre on a dark background is characteristic and this carpet also has the motifs of the swans and the flowing ribbon. Directoire period.

54   Savonnerie carpet. 18th century. Catan Collection, Paris.

55 Savonnerie carpet. 18th century. Musée National, Versailles.

56 Savonnerie carpet (detail). Early 19th century. Catan Collection, Paris.

contact with them, and the harmonious curves which from then onwards dominated all aspects of French decorative art appeared in furniture and found a corresponding element in carpets. This unmistakable, elegantly rounded quality, based on skilfully interwoven, apparently frivolous motifs, was the basis of the development from one to the next of the various styles called Baroque, Rococo, Louis XVI, Directoire, Empire, Restoration, Louis Philippe, Second Empire and finally Art Nouveau.

At all periods and in all styles carpet design in France matched the decoration of Boulle furniture, made from ebony inlaid with tortoiseshell, often enriched with carved gilt bronze. Some of this furniture was lacquered in that famous dark red colour that provided a background for exotic figures in oriental style; there were carved and gilded 'consoles' and wall tables; carved and lacquered wainscotting; carved walnut tables with elegant volutes; rosewood cabinets with coloured woods; marquetry decorated chests of drawers and small tables with scenes executed with the individual type of perspective peculiar to it. The motifs and colouring of French carpets are also found in white and gold lacquer work, and in the medallions of Sèvres porcelain encased in valuable wood on cabinets, small tables and writing desks. The same fine curves as in the designs of carpets occur in the brackets and supports made in the shape of swans, and the same sphinxes of the 'Retour d'Egypte'. It is worth repeating that all these decorative aspects of French furniture derive from French carpets, which played such a large part in the arts of France from the 17th to the 19th century.

Such painters as Oudry, La Tour, Boucher, Watteau, Audran, Chardin, Nattier and Fragonard designed tapestries and carpets. Their works inspired such expert carvers and furniture-makers as Delanois, Delorme, Cressent, Leleu, Petit and Oeben, as well as the famous sculptors and casters in bronze, the Slodtz brothers, who did not think it beneath them to design furniture, candlesticks and other articles for use in the house.

Marie Antoinette realised that French carpets could be a source by which German furniture might be ennobled and enhanced. For this reason she called German craftsmen in wood to the French court so that they could learn the two greatest gifts of the French mind: restraint and balance.

Savonnerie. So-called Savonnerie carpets still exist today, produced by the Manufacture d'Etat de la Savonnerie—the same organisation as the Manufacture Royale de la Savonnerie set up in 1663 under Louis XIV. But its origins go back to the workshops set up beneath the Galerie du Louvre by Pierre Dupont. This first workshop, as already mentioned, produced '*Tapis à la façon du Levant et à la façon de la Turquie*'. Dupont had the acumen to recognise the

57 Savonnerie carpet. 19th century. Catan Collection, Paris.

58 Savonnerie carpet (detail). 19th century. Catan Collection, Paris.

57   Savonnerie carpet. 19th century. Catan Collection, Paris.
An example made for Marshal Ney; it includes the sword and
the baton of a Marshal of France. The geometrical design is a
symptom of decadence. Empire period.

58   Savonnerie carpet (detail). 19th century. Catan Collection, Paris. Blue and dark red are the dominant colours in this
carpet; the double borders with typical floral motifs and the
garlands in the four corners are expressive. Empire period.

59   Savonnerie carpet (detail). 19th century. Private collection, Milan. This example is characterised by very rich
decoration in which garlands and bunches of flowers predominate. Borders of leaves outline the medallion and run
along the edge. The main colours are yellow and blue.

59 Savonnerie carpet (detail). 19th century.

gifts of his employee Simon Lourdet, and made him his partner.

In 1627 Dupont and Lourdet installed themselves in an abandoned building which had at one time been a soapworks. The name 'Savonnerie' comes from the French word *savon,* meaning soap. Louis XIII (1610–1643) was pleased by this initiative and granted the partners a concession of eighteen years for the production of 'Levantine carpets and creations'; a school of weaving and knotting was also set up for orphans and poor children. Later this school became a primarily philanthropic organisation, financed with money assigned to the older boys—who had to pay it to the orphanage in return for their keep—for the work they did. The King also rewarded the partners with a patent of nobility, guaranteeing them an income and granting other privileges.

Differences arose between the partners, and as a result they thereafter worked separately: Dupont continued as director in the Galerie du Louvre, while Lourdet took sole responsibility for Savonnerie production.

Early Savonnerie production was quite varied and included screens, panels, tapestry, firescreens, chair covers, etc., as well as carpets. Within a few years production had increased enormously; the workshop finally became exclusively devoted to carpets, one reason being Louis XIII's prohibition of the importation of Eastern carpets. The differences between Pierre Dupont and Simon Lourdet had hardly any influence on the quality or quantity of production, which became of national importance.

Savonnerie still had one point of contact with Eastern carpets: the use of the Ghiordes knot. In every other respect the technique was completely different. The warp and weft were almost always in hemp and the pile in wool. One feature of Savonnerie knotting is the method used to cut the threads of the wool pile. Instead of each knot being cut separately, a row of knots was threaded on to a thin iron bar with one end shaped like the blade of a knife, and all the threads were cut at once. The same technique was used in making velvet. Dyes with a vegetable base were used to colour the wool.

The Gobelins factory

In 1662 one of Louis XIV's ministers, Colbert, set up the Manufacture Royale des Gobelins, whose production was exclusively devoted to tapestry and fabrics for covering chairs, canopies, etc. Colbert also gave the Savonnerie factory a new constitution, joining it with Gobelins and placing it under the direction of the *'Premier Peintre du Roi'*, Charles Lebrun. Henceforth the master weavers had nothing to do but supervise the technical processes involved in the execution of the carpets and teach the boys; once a month a painter from the Royal Academy made a tour of inspection, putting forward new designs and models. As a result, carpets became more French in feeling than ever, expressing perfectly the French Baroque style which was to be imitated in so many other European countries.

Orders for the palaces of the Louvre and the Tuileries poured in, and all the workshops scattered about the circumference of Paris, and all those depending on the Savonnerie, were extremely active. This was the period of carpets with garlands and posies of flowers standing out against dark backgrounds; such designs matched superbly the ebony furniture inlaid with floral motifs. There were also examples woven in silk, gold and silver; the oldest were not as big as carpets preserved in museums today, which are all made of wool and are of large dimensions.

It was during the reign of Louis XIV that the thirteen carpets in the Gallery of Apollo in the Louvre were woven, as were the other ninety-three in the same palace and those made for the Grande Chambre du Roi and the throne room in the Palace of the Tuileries. In addition, of course, there were the carpets that Louis XIV had made in order to give to the sovereigns, ambassadors and nobles of other countries.

The tapestry designer Baudrin Yvart, and François Francart, a designer of *objets d'art,* were also important, preparing designs of great refinement for Savonnerie carpets. The following specialists also deserve to be mentioned: Monnoyer (flowers), Boel (animals), and Genoel (landscapes).

The curving lines which characterise the Baroque and, later, the Rococo style (which contained even more curves) dominate the design of the Savonnerie carpet too.

Between the elegant curves linking garlands and posies of flowers together against a dark background there are often landscapes or allegories in the corners of the carpets. They are skilfully executed in different shades of the same colour, creating an effect like that of a bas relief. The centre of the carpet always contains a meaningful figurative motif, either the globe or the head of Apollo (clearly symbolic of the Sun King). The elements of the composition are not very varied but are endlessly and ingeniously permutated. The genius of the artist is revealed in the inventive quality of the decoration. Naturalistic motifs are used to 'place' the carpets, which were often destined for particular houses or people. Hunting, war or mythological scenes are often combined with symbolism referring to the king; sometimes there is an open allusion to his greatness. And always there is a profusion of surrounding flowers and scrolls apparently intended to imitate the fluttering of feathers. The result is an exuberant triumph of creative design and skilful workmanship.

60 Savonnerie carpet (detail). Early 19th century. Malmaison.

61 Bidjar carpet (detail). Second half of the 19th century. Private collection, Milan.

60   Savonnerie carpet (detail). Early 19th century. Malmaison. In the oval centre, which has a frame with yellow
bees on a white background, the Napoleonic 'N'. The light
background of the carpet makes the multi-coloured feathers
and the laurel border, themes which often occurred at this
period, stand out.

61   Bidjar carpet (detail). Second half of the 19th century.
Private collection, Milan. This carpet was made in Persia, but
the commission and design were French. Both the motif,
which is repeated all over the field, and the border, which
looks like petit point, are definitely of French inspiration.

62   Aubusson carpet (detail). First half of the 19th century.
Catan Collection, Paris. In this example one notices the
mixture of geometrical and floral designs which was typical
of this period of stylistic transition.

63   Aubusson carpet (detail). 18th century. Private collection, Milan. The multi-coloured and elegant decoration unfurls
on a light background. The blue and the typical laurel-leaf
border held together by bows can be distinguished in the
decoration.

62 Aubusson carpet (detail). First half of the 19th century.
Catan Collection, Milan.

At the end of the 17th century Savonnerie experienced a temporary set-back because of financial difficulties and the closing of the Gobelins in 1699. Early in the 18th century the Duc d'Antin enabled the Savonnerie to resume work on a large scale and face the competition of Aubusson. In the meantime taste and fashion changed, influenced by the famous architect Robert de Cotte, who introduced less curved lines of an elegance that was less ostentatious. A new elegance characterised polite society in France during the 18th century, pervading everything from clothing to *objets d'art*.

In this new period of great activity the Savonnerie factory continued to produce for the royal family. The building of the palace of Versailles meant a demand for carpets to adorn the throne room, the bedrooms of the King and Queen, the Chapel with the altar, the nave, the royal pulpit, and the private chapels of the Queen, the King's daughters and the Dauphin's wife. Later came commissions for the execution of carpets for the King's banqueting room, the council chamber, the banqueting room at the Trianon (the delightful pavilion in the park of Versailles), for the Dauphine's bedroom, the King's private study, the gaming room, and the King's private apartments.

Orders followed for the château of Fontainebleau:

63 Aubusson carpet (detail). 18th century. Private collection, Milan.

apartments for the King and Queen, the Chapel, and so on. Other royal residences, for example the château of Choisy, La Muette, Bellevue, St Hubert and Marly, were decorated—and carpeted—in turn. And all the time orders were given for ceremonial carpets for foreign monarchs.

The painters who drew designs for Savonnerie carpets at this time were Belin de Fontenay (a 'flower-painter' and pupil of Monnoyer), and his collaborator Pierre Josse Perrot, 'painter of ornaments'. Fontenay was François Boucher's master for tapestry design, and Gravelot's and Chevillon's for carpets. The sensitive and refined flower designs which played such a part in the success of Savonnerie carpets were the creation of Louis Tessier and Maurice Jacques. These carpets were no longer called '*à la façon du Levant*' but '*tapis veloutés*', a definition which is entirely appropriate. The backgrounds were now worked in bright colours, on which were set the most varied types of flowers, interspersed with other ornamental motifs. Most of these carpets bear the king's arms, dominated by the crown and the sacred insignia, and flanked by the palm of victory and two great eagles' wings extended; this design was created by the genius of Perrot.

Towards the middle of the 18th century a taste for the classical developed, although the curvilinear design and the floral surround were retained. There was also a brief return to the Louis XIV style, and there are copies of carpets made in his time for the Great Gallery in the Louvre. They are huge and brilliantly coloured. Sometimes two or three copies were made of the same design—for example the three identical carpets made for the king's pulpit in the palace of Versailles. The carpet made in 1727 for the base of the royal throne at Versailles was copied at least twice, in 1761 and 1770, always for the same purpose. And a carpet made from a design by Perrot in 1735 for the banqueting hall in La Muette was copied in 1740 for Choisy and in 1769 for Fontainebleau.

Royal mistresses were important patrons of the arts. Whatever their motives—pride, love of luxury, ostentation—Madame de Montespan, mistress of Louis XIV, and Mesdames de Pompadour and du Barry, mistresses of Louis XV, loved to surround themselves with beautiful things. Classical and Arcadian scenes appeared on tapestry and carpets and were then taken up and reproduced in miniatures, divan covers and murals. Porcelain developed along the same lines and its incomparable decorations complemented carpet designs perfectly.

The manufacture of Savonnerie carpets continued without interruption during the reigns of Louis XV (1715–1774) and Louis XVI (1774–1792). At the same time as Louis XV carpets were being copied, Marie Antoinette, Louis XVI's queen, introduced the taste for antique and exotic subjects into France.

64 Aubusson carpet. 18th century. Catan Collection, Paris.

65 Aubusson carpet (detail). 19th century. Private collection, Milan.

64   Aubusson carpet. 18th century. Catan Collection, Paris.
The decoration in light colours stands out in elegant fashion
against the dark background of the centre and the dark blue
of the field. The motif on the borders echoes that of the centre.
Louis XVI period.

65   Aubusson carpet (detail). 19th century. Private collection, Milan. This carpet is elongated, and the vaguely geometrical design, executed in extremely delicate colours, is in
harmony with the shape. Second Empire period.

66   Aubusson carpet (detail). 19th century. Private collection, Milan. The Second Empire did not renounce the delicacy
of design characteristic of the preceding century. Here the
light colours are very skilfully fused together.

67   Aubusson carpet (detail). First half of the 19th century.
Private collection, Milan. This was made for the Russian Court,
marked 'Manufacture Royale d'Aubusson des Chevaliers
Sallandrouze Lamornaix'. It is woven in silk and wool and
the ornamentation is emphasised by the use of gold and
silver; it manages to express French and Russian taste at one
and the same time, and creates a bizarre and sumptuous effect.

66 Aubusson carpet (detail). 19th century. Private collection, Milan.

As a result, flambeaux, cornucopias and helmets appear on carpets, juxtaposed with Chinese parasols, crescent moons and strings of pearls; and in the borders key-patterns are found next to Roman ruins. This motif owed its popularity to the excavations at Pompeii and Herculaneum, and in the Roman Forum, which began in the second half of the 18th century and were an important factor in the development of Neo-classicism. In homage perhaps to the buried past which was being brought into the light, the colours used in the decoration became more delicate.

At the end of the century prices of Savonnerie carpets were so high that orders fell, and in order to maintain production inferior materials were used and the designs became poorer. The Revolution of 1789 gave a new impetus to carpet production. Directoire carpets had simpler designs with less flowing lines and fewer colours. In these years the carpets produced at Aubusson improved in quality and offered Savonnerie carpets strong competition.

The 19th century

The fortunes of Savonnerie revived with the foundation of the Napoleonic Empire: a new court, a new aristocracy, a massive programme of building, and

67 Aubusson carpet (detail). First half of the 19th century. Private collection, Milan.

national expansion meant a great increase in the demand for carpets and other items of interior decoration. The Savonnerie factory was now called the Manufacture Nationale des Tapis et Meubles façon de Perse dits Savonnerie, and orders poured into it.

The architects Percier and Fontaine had the task of rearranging the Napoleonic residences and repairing the damage sustained by the great palaces during the Revolution. It was necessary to restore much that had been destroyed and looted, and the Savonnerie worked for the Tuileries, Versailles, St Cloud, and Compiègne. The designers worked together, preparing design upon design for the new carpets; the most important were Lagrenée, Dugourc, La Hamayade de Saint-Ange (appointed designer of the Mobilier Impérial in 1810), Dubois and Devertu. The Empire style, like all preceding French styles, followed a fixed set of rules to which everything had to be adapted. The Napoleonic symbols (the N, the eagle, the Imperial crowns, etc.) predominate, in frames which are no longer curving and between garlands of flowers depicted with more restraint than those of the Baroque period. Classical motifs were an essential part of the Empire style, and Egyptian motifs became popular as a result of the Napoleonic campaigns in Egypt.

The most active designer was Saint-Ange, who continued his work without interruption after the fall of Napoleon, through the reigns of Louis XVIII (1814–1824), Charles X (1824–1830) and Louis Philippe (1830–1848). In each period he was able to strike the right note and use the appropriate decoration, adapting the symbols of each sovereign without foregoing the basic qualities of restraint, good taste and elegance. Colours became more intense and the famous brilliant red that gives individuality to the carpets of this period makes its appearance.

In May 1825 Savonnerie and Gobelins were again amalgamated and transferred to the same place. In 1826 there was another move, to the site on the banks of the river Bièvre, where the Savonnerie works is still located.

The Second Empire (1852–1870) was another era of intensive carpet-making to meet the demands of the state. Carpets of the previous régimes had to be maintained and new carpets made with the insignia and monograms of the new sovereigns, Napoleon III and the Empress Eugénie. The Empress shared the ambition and love of elegance that had characterised so many past consorts and royal mistresses, and was as anxious as her husband to acquire furnishings consonant with her dignity. At this time the backgrounds of the carpets were executed in brilliant and varied colours (yellows, reds, greens), though there was a brief return to dark backgrounds. The floral tradition continued, and bouquets of flowers and garlands appear repeatedly as Leitmotifs. Such

68 Aubusson carpet (detail). Second half of the 19th century. Private collection, Milan.

69 Aubusson carpet. End of the 18th century. Private collection, Milan.

68   Aubusson carpet (detail). Second half of the 19th century. Private collection, Milan. A carpet characteristic of the period; rich and well-spaced designs which stand out from the green of the background in strong contrast to the purplish colour of the outside border.

69   Aubusson carpet. End of the 18th century. Private collection, Milan. The olive-green colour of the field is extremely beautiful and brings out the simple but elegant central decoration in light colours.

70   Dutch carpet. End of the 17th century. Tarica Collection, Paris. This is an extremely rare, if not unique, carpet of its type; in fact Holland made no contribution of note to the art of carpet-making. This one deserves attention because of its rarity. In the centre, on a yellow background, is a heraldic crest with the symbolism of a ladder, an anchor and sea-horses. The decoration of the field and borders is of the typical *mille fleurs* type, refined and extremely elegant.

70 Dutch carpet. End of the 17th century. Tarica Collection, Paris.

motifs are found in all French carpets, even in this, the century of Romanticism.

Typical of Romantic taste—in carpets as in other things—was a delight in Medieval settings. Castles, ruins, trophies, mountain-tops, panoplies, arranged artistically within a border of rich and attractive vegetation, were combined to create the romantic atmosphere in which the legends of the great Medieval lovers were presented: Tristan and Iseult, Pelleas and Melisande, Ugo and Parisina move about among garlands of flowers and rose petals that are scattered everywhere.

The fall of the Second Empire in 1870 had little effect on French carpet production, which continued to be financed by the state. At present the Savonnerie works is a part of the Mobilier National, which takes care of state residences, ministries, embassies, etc. Copies of old models are still made, and although modern production never equals the achievements of the past, it still expresses that refinement of taste which demands surroundings of harmony and elegance.

Aubusson. Aubusson is a small town in central France which has for centuries been a centre of tapestry-making by local craftsmen. In 1665 Colbert amalgamated local producers into the Manufacture de Tapisserie, giving the industry, which until then had been in private hands, a kind of official status.

From this time Aubusson tapestries were signed MRDA, which stands for Manufacture Royale d'Aubusson. In spite of the new high-sounding name, the tapestries did not improve greatly, and always remained inferior to those of Gobelins, Beauvais, and other great French factories. But if Aubusson tapestries were inferior in quality and accuracy of execution, they created an effect of great spontaneity and bore the unmistakable stamp of the personality of the executant. Aubusson tapestries were made for provincial customers and private individuals of modest means. They lacked the stateliness and pomp of tapestries made for the court but all the same had the merit of immediacy.

During the second half of the 18th century the Aubusson carpet developed from tapestry work. The same technique was used in working the carpets as had been employed for tapestry, apart from a few variations of Eastern origin. The execution was similar to that of the Caucasian Soumak carpets. In Aubusson carpets the work was carried out on a loom, the surface being worked by means of shuttles on the prepared warp. As in Soumak carpets, the surface emerged smooth and the threads with which it had been worked hung down on the reverse side. The oldest examples were made completely in wool, on a hemp or cotton warp.

Unlike the tapestries, in which the design was always figurative, with narrative pictures or portraits, Aubusson carpets were objects complete in themselves, pictures being replaced by a few details, such as monograms and armorial bearings. Aubusson designs have an architectural quality and sometimes look like exact copies of ceilings, reproducing stucco effects and panels with skilful shading. Sometimes these carpets were even placed directly on the ceiling, which created an atmosphere that was aristocratic and extremely unusual.

The stylistic evolution of Aubusson carpets closely follows that of Savonnerie. They are less important, since the weave is less strong, but the nobility and grace of the designs and colours have no superior. In spite of their relative lack of durability, Aubusson carpets were commissioned and made according to precise instructions as to size and shape. They were then fixed to the ground to prevent wrinkling—which explains the numbers sometimes found along the edges of old Aubussons. These numbers were stamped on so that the carpet could be aligned with the walls and furniture.

The decoration is as good as that of Savonnerie carpets. Savonnerie was always valued more highly, but there were nonetheless times when Aubussons were of a higher quality. This happened during the crises which afflicted Savonnerie production in the late 17th and late 18th centuries. The Aubussons, which were less expensive and less internationally known, were then sold to French buyers who lacked either the desire or the money to order from abroad. In this way the production of Aubusson, which had mainly consisted of wall- and furniture-covers, hangings and canopies, was given over entirely to carpets. In the periods of most intense activity the Aubusson looms created masterpieces in wool, silk, gold and silver. Threads laminated in gold and silver came into use, whence the term '*lamé*'.

The most important Aubusson carpets were made in the first half of the 19th century, including examples commissioned by foreign royalty. The carpet reproduced in plate 67, for example, was ordered by the Russian Imperial court in the early years of the century. This carpet is outstanding because of its unusual decorative composition; motifs which are decidedly Russian in design and colour are superimposed on French motifs with complete success. Entirely French is the flight of colourful birds, each one different from the rest, which circles round the centre, on a green background with olive branches. Gold and silver embellish the decoration and create a fantastical and unusual effect. Many other carpets deserve to be mentioned, but they are difficult to find; owing to the weakness of the weave, they perish more quickly than Savonnerie carpets.

The variety of sizes produced adds to the value of Aubusson carpets, which were made in response to many different types of demand. Whereas Savonnerie produced only for the state and mainly furnished

great palaces, Aubusson always supplied a wider
public. This variety and adaptability is one of the
great charms of the Aubusson carpet.